ESSENSE

Brie Forde

ESSENSE © 2024 Brie Forde

All rights reserved.

No part of this publication may be reproduced, stored in a retrieval system, or transmitted, in any form or by any means, electronic, mechanical, photocopying, recording, or otherwise, without the prior written permission of the presenters.

Brie Forde asserts the moral right to be identified as the author of this work.

Presentation by *BookLeaf Publishing*

Web: www.bookleafpub.com

E-mail: info@bookleafpub.com

ISBN: 9789358367645

First edition 2024

*These poems are yours - may we live in the truest es**sense** of ourselves, not holding back anything. Let us embody all of our **senses** in becoming all that we are meant to be.*

This book is dedicated to all the beautiful souls of this earth. May your path be guided by light and love always.

ACKNOWLEDGEMENTS

I would like to thank every single person who has come along on this journey with me. Without you all, I wouldn't be where I am today. I would like to thank my beautiful family for always pushing me to create, for always seeing the light within me, and encouraging me to shine. You all have touched my heart in a multitude of ways.

This is for us.

Inside Me

I have run away so often they stopped searching
for me. I stopped searching for myself. And you
can't make yourself disappear that simple. I
watch the tears run down my face like a
marathon, but I should be grateful because the
sun is still shining, right? The storm made it on
the other side of town, right?

But I am still running, still escaping, still hiding
from me. I thought to myself, how can anyone
love both the brightest and darkest parts of me if
I am the natural disaster? I don't want to be in
this body to escape. I do not want to be with you
for mere comfort. I am not meant to keep hiding,
keep running, or keep quiet. I know the rainbow
is out there.

Abyss

I watch the rain pour itself into soil and think, how deep is this dirt? Is this soil even permeable? Is the rain even breaking through? Maybe this soil (soul) is too hard. Maybe, asking a dead thing to breathe again was a mistake.

- *Maybe the difference between the soil and a soul is u and i.*

Sun + Moon

There is nothing I wish to change about my appearance when I have my father's smile and my mother's hands.

-     *Two halves make me whole*

Transparent

I like to believe that in another lifetime, I am entirely me. Not hiding in the shadows, closets, and corners of my life. That I am who I am meant to be. That I know I am the love of my life and I complete myself.

- *I am trying to be that here in this lifetime.*

I Am The Prize

5

And I will love all the tender parts of me.
I will tell my inner critic, "You are wrong, again.
How dare you try and trick me into believing I
am anything other than extraordinary."

-    *First place*

Present

All I ask for is your smile.
A simple gesture to let me know that I am
safe within the gaps of your teeth.
And I will ask for your hand.
Like a book I am opening up for the first time.
I want to read your palms and all the
secrets you bury inside.
And I will ask for your love.
The pulse of your heartbeat
is like the consistency of the ocean's waves.
You give me unwavering patience.
You give me steadiness.
You give me it all in one.

-    *Tangible or not, you have always given*
     me you.

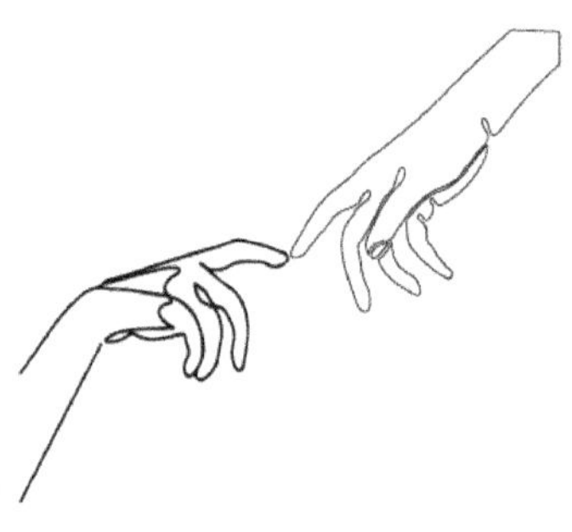

Yours

And you chose me.
Out of all the rhythms in this world,
We are the melodies for each other.
It is as if Cupid stopped playing match-
maker to listen to the symphonies of our
hearts. And when we love, it is loud. You are
like the last breath I take before I dive into the
ocean, *deep*. I cannot live in love without you
and our song.

And where would we be without the pain?
Without the hurt? Without the mistakes?
Learning with and from you is the greatest gift a
partner could treasure. To be by the side of the
person whom I love. To watch them be watered
DAILY in love, in vulnerability, in consistency,
and truth.

You tell me how you became like magic. How
you are so rare and I want to know how you
make love look so easy. You make love so
breathtaking; and when we make love, it is
beautiful and nurturing. The seeds of our garden
are held with such gentleness. I have never
grown so tender.

A year and counting with you and I have learned
to be selfless again. I have learned to let my
petals bloom and let my roots reach the earth
again and again and again. You have shown me
how to reach for the sun every single day, even
when it is not in sight. You have shown me how
to be so full like the moon and to embrace all my
phases and stages. Thankfulness isn't enough,
but I do thank God for you, everyday.

And I cannot make this up, you are perfect. You
make me see the beautiful colors inside of
myself. I am your bee, your heart is a sunflower,
and I am attracted to what makes you bright.
The honey I make is as sweet as your smile. I
am afraid to dip my lips in, so I watch; I linger
and wait for your voice to give the okay, but
there is no swaying; no movement of wind, no
rushing the first taste of our love and this is the
most patient I've been all season. No more
rushing into spring; teach me how to bloom
flowers you have sowed into my heart.

Under the Weather and Rainbow

I struggle to talk about my sexuality
Like I am choking on air.
In the springtime, I have allergies.
When I am in love, I get the stomach bug and
throw up all of the reasons
I like to think I might not be gay.
And my nose is constantly running
out of excuses, much like me every time
I have to explain my sexuality to those
that fear it.

I want to stop giving an alias whenever my
therapist asks about you. I mean, what do I even
say "Uhhhhhh, actually Ellen, I'm in love
with a girl and have been for the past
year and a half," but I can't just explain
That to her. She'd probably say, "NO WAY!
This changes EVERYTHING!" And I'd
say, "No, it does not!" Does my love mean
anything less now because it is for a
woman? Is what I've told you all these months
now meaningless because you can't relate to it?
Do you think I am a terrible person?

Incapable of loving another human being who happens to be another woman, yet is still a human?

But instead, I shrug and give her half of a smile because I can only tell her half of the truth, and I say, "me and 'Josh' are doing just fine."

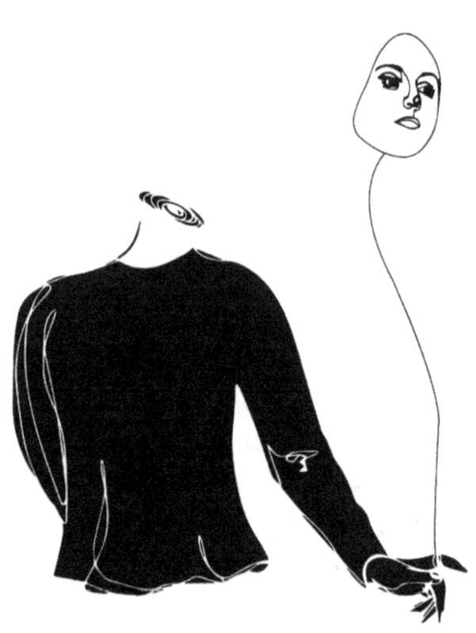

I Am My One True Love

I thought to myself, if I have gone a day without
laughter, I have truly spent it in waste.
I also thought about love. And how often I think
about it. And how often I write about it. I think
about the feeling before love. Because love
alone does not produce the euphoric feelings
I've experienced. Joy was there and will be there
after love is gone. Then I thought to myself,
what is love if not parallel to freedom?
And what's parallel to freedom if not
expression? I think about the times love has
swept me away, and the times it has cut my rope
in half. It was my mistake for believing it could
hold up everything that embodied me. But I have
learned that I am merely, realistically, simply,
more than the exceptional and conceptual idea of
love. I express it, I give it freely, but I hold
power and passion in my eyes too. My hands
have touched the earth more times than my
scraped knees can count. My hips have danced
loudly and gracefully with the rhythms of the
wind. My legs have carried me home multiple
times to tone-deaf bodies, mistakable lovers, and
captivating places, but it has always led the way
back to the roadmaps between my thighs.

Envy

My therapist hands me a sheet of
paper for homework and says, "I want you to
practice noticing your emotions for the next two
weeks." If you know anything about me, you
know that I wear my feelings like a coat and
allow myself to freeze in the winter. But I will
give and give to make sure every living soul
next to me is not dying; that their hearts are kept
warm and I ask myself is this selfish?
Is this toxic? Does my body envy me
because I don't know what it's like
to be everyone else I put before me? When will I
learn that I must come first and that if I am not
aggressive with this truth, I will think that every
person who sympathizes with me is compatible.

Eclipse

I thank the day for giving me the night.
This pledge to come back tomorrow.
I thank the day for shining its glow,
ever so gently on the moon's back
which has been carrying our
darkest deeds for centuries.
It too, sees where humanity has
got it all wrong.

We choose to love these entities
separately as if they are not in the
arches of our heels and in the
posture of our smiles. They are
never late, yet they are never
holding hands.

How lonely it must be. Everyday
chasing after one another, yet they
wait centuries to meet in the middle.

Elemental

Instead of arguing with the thunder,
I allow myself to watch the lightning.
I let myself sit. Pause. Ponder with
the emotions I don't allow myself to
feel. The ones I hide from everyone.
I do not look directly at the lightning,
and I wonder if that is a bad thing.
I wonder if not sitting in comfortability
makes it any easier to sit in silence.

I don't numb the pain anymore.
I don't make excuses for all the times
the lightning has struck the ground,
or struck me.
I simply let it be and allow myself to feel every
bit of emotion the earth expresses.
I don't let it hold back.

-    *I wouldn't want to either.*

What they don't teach us in grade school

I am unlearning the science of myself. I am slowly unfolding the genetic makeup of this body and giving myself a new universe. I cannot live where the moon and sun are not seen.

- *Solar System*

Renaissance

Blooming beauty, do not take shelter. I know the
skies seem gloom and gray and all you want is
to fall apart, but you mustn't. After the rain falls,
you must get back up. For you are a flower, your
mind is a garden, and the rain makes you
beautiful. Withstanding the wind, water, and
ways of mother earth's cycles, you are magic.

The rain is merely a rebirth, a reset, an
awakening of the strength inside of you.
Lightning strikes your soil to ignite that
passionate fire within you.

Roots

The flowers are sitting on the lap of my window sill, the clouds linger, yet it is still a beautiful day. Jealous of the glass space between them, they asked me,

"Why don't we get to feel the sunrise? Why must we be separated from the wind? Why have I not breathed in the soil of the earth I was created in?"

> \- *I cried and thought about the opportunities we've been deprived of.*

Numb

I feel as if I am a weeping willow tree that can't stop its roots from drowning. Everything is too much and too little and not enough. I'm barely surviving and this garden just feels empty. This summer is not the same. I am not the same and I do not know how to deal with this version of me. I hate this garden and sometimes I even hate myself. I know hate is the evilest act one can commit, but lately I feel like I've been betrayed. Been lied to. Been wrongly accused, taken for granted, and this is still just my body. I can't even tell you about everything on my mind. The conversation always ends in you and how you're doing good. Right now I am not good. Right now I am not here. Right now, I don't want to be alive in a body that makes me feel dead.

Fluttering

I never know what to say when you
make me feel important. I never know
how to hold the compliments you give me.

-　　*Like a butterfly, I let it go.*

Conditional

I do not think I am meant for everyone. I think I am supposed to be a one-way flight. A lost city. A deserted island that is at peace with being alone and this body, well this body. What can I say other than I'm still surviving in it, right?

- *When will I be good enough for me?*

Sometimes, I too forget

Sometimes, I get so bothered going back and forth with the thoughts in my head I start to forget which one's my voice. I get so warped in time that I forget another sunset has gone by. I forget to take that minute to stare at the clouds. To watch them wave at me as they cross the big blue and beautiful sky. Sometimes, I forget too much, but I do remember to smile.

Freedom

I can no longer fault my ancestors.
I too now know what it must be like
To see the fruit ripening in front of me.
To see it dangling from the tree.
To envision the tiniest bite of something
that you can't even call yours.
It was like I was intoxicated,
not with your love, but with desire.
I kept thinking of what could happen
And what I wanted to happen.
But if I had trusted my desire, I wouldn't
be any different from them.

-    I cannot be both the gardener and weeds

Aquarius

The earth dug its roots into my mother
and she birthed me in the middle of
a solar eclipse. I am half sun, half moon, whole
universe. I don't apologize for the thunder in
my voice anymore. I don't apologize for
conceiving tsunamis when I am grieving. I don't
apologize for the volcanic eruptions I hold in my
fists. I only apologize for the disasters I have
caused without warning.

Self Portrait

Your power is merely contained in the essense of how you love your soul, and the way you show others how to.

-    *A mirror is held to your heart*

Essesnse

I am hiding behind the curtains of the sky. The clouds know I am here, yet I am not always seen by the world. Some days are much harder than others. Some days, my rays give you a glimpse of where I am when I don't know my own location and some days, I don't even bother to stretch my hand. Some days, I am so distracted by the noise of the thunder, that I don't even bother coming out.

But when I dance in the midst of the rain, the earth is much softer, brighter, and lighter. When I dance in the midst of the rain, I don't apologize for bringing the earth two gifts. I don't apologize for healing what humans have destroyed so carelessly. Do you see what happens when the light touches something that is meant to be reflected? When we dance in the midst of the rain, right there is the rainbow.

What I have learned from loving you:

<u>The danger I find in myself:</u>

If I am not careful, I will put you on a pedestal and forget myself. I will let you reign, becoming the sun and the moon of my galaxy;

everything will revolve around you. I will learn to let go of the things that first taught me how to love: poetry, art, and nature.

I will wake up every morning not craving an appetite, but your presence. I will forget to hold my own hand, and reach for yours.

26

<u>The safety I find in myself:</u>

I have appreciated God for allowing our paths to cross. I have loved watching you listen to me with your entire being; you listen with purpose.

I have loved hearing you speak about everything that captivates you to grow; you have helped me breathe life into my passions again.

I have loved hearing your heart on countless occasions; not just from the beating of your chest, but in the way you show love to others. You have helped me to shine the universe within myself. You have loved me outside of time, in a continuous period; there are no intervals when we are away.

An ode to diversity

I am listening. To the voices of brave souls, the ones who have walked down a road before me, I am here. I am present in their pain.
I acknowledge my own heritage and how my ancestors held the light for me to be enlightened. I hold the candle of awareness and see that we are all at the busy intersection of a crossroad. I am speaking for them. they say to us, let us slow down the speed of our bias. Let us not erode away at the beauty of others when we meet. Let us not see past the warning sign up ahead. An intersection is a plus sign so may we be cautioned to see this addition, and not sigh. Not hold breath, nor waste space but hold it for all that are welcomed. May the stop sign be an octagon of authenticity. Let it allow us all to pause and look internally. At our preconceived opinions about one another. May it hold a mirror, to all of the places and spaces in need of an abrupt halt. May diversity, inclusion, and equality be the green light and never the red. May the crosswalk not countdown against those who have been waiting years to walk in freedom. May we see each pedestrian as ourself and give caution to all that have every right of way.

GrateFULL

The wind woke me up this morning with its
gentle whisper in my ear. My head, resting near
the window, eyes gazing towards the clouds.
It said,

"Today, I will not miss the sun. I have
the wind in my corner, the breath
of the earth in my laughter, and its core
foundation in my smile."

I am capable of loving myself

the way I love others

I want to caress love in the palm of my hands
and allow its warmth to spread;
like sunlight touching the earth at sunrise.

I want to hear its heartbeat, memorize the
melody like a song on a continuous loop, and
record all of the moments it takes my breath
away.

www.ingramcontent.com/pod-product-compliance
Lightning Source LLC
LaVergne TN
LVHW010949200726
843509LV00013B/2333